THE LIVING NATIVITY

By Helen Haidle

Illustrated by David Haidle

Honor Books
Tulsa, Oklahoma

To
Curt and Pam Peters
Remembering Christmas in Germany 1969:
God brought us together in the little farm-village of Grenzhof.

And in appreciation to
Stan Sposito
And other faithful friends who posed for the illustrations:
Louie, Melissa, Tim, and Brittany Nigro;
Mike and Penny O'Hearn; Keith, Judy, Amy, Ryan, and Joy Reetz;
David Spinosa, Josh Spinosa, Kelby Smith, Linley Shepherd,
Chemi Wambalaba, and Royce Williams.

And to
Jeannie Taylor and Barbara Martin
You are *gifts* from God to us.
This book is better because of you!

The Living Nativity
ISBN 1-56292-537-7
Copyright ©1998 David & Helen Haidle
4190 S.W. 195th Ct.
Beaverton, Oregon 97007

Published by Honor Books, Inc.
P.O. Box 55388
Tulsa, Oklahoma 74155

THE STORY OF SAINT FRANCIS
&
THE CHRISTMAS MANGER

by

David & Helen Haidle

In 1223 A.D. when Saint Francis of Assisi created the first known crèche—a real-life reenactment of Christ's birth—it was done in Greccio, a small Italian town near Assisi. Saint Francis' dramatic re-creation of the first nativity helped people catch a new vision of the birth of Jesus Christ.

We do know that this event was held on the mountainside overlooking the town of Greccio. We do not know the exact details of what Saint Francis did. Some writings say it began very simply—with the Holy Family, an ox, and a donkey. Additional animals, shepherds, etc., were said to be used in the following years. We also know that this custom spread to other cities in Italy and then into the rest of Europe.

Knowing Francis' love for children, animals, and most of all, his Lord Jesus Christ, the first reenactment might have happened something like this . . .

Antonio limped up the dusty road leading out of the village. Tears smudged his face while his eyes anxiously scanned the hillside.

"Benito! Benito! Where are you?" he called as he stopped to rub his painful foot. "I never do anything right," he muttered. "Why did I forget to latch the stable door again? Now it's getting too dark to find him. And I can't run any farther."

A friendly voice called out, "The Lord be with you."

The boy quickly wiped the tears from his eyes.

The stranger came closer. "What brings you out here at night?"

"I lost my master's donkey," said Antonio, hanging his head.

The man wearing a monk's robe chuckled. "I think I found him!"

Antonio looked up, "Benito! Oh, thank you, Sir."

"I'm Brother Francis and I'm afraid that your donkey is hurt."

Antonio's heart pounded. "My master will be angry," he groaned.

The monk spoke reassuringly. "If you pull out the briars and clean the wounds, all will be well. Let's get back to your stable."

Walking down the road, Antonio caught the scent of smoke from a shepherd's fire in the nearby pasture. Brother Francis abruptly stopped.

"Ohh!" he said softly. "This looks like Bethlehem that first Christmas Eve. Imagine how the shepherds felt when the angel appeared and told them, *'Fear not! For unto you is born this day a Savior, who is Christ the Lord.'* And imagine hearing thousands of angels praise God!"

Brother Francis put his arm around Antonio's shoulder. "God sent His Son to become one of us. Do *you* understand what that means, my friend?"

Shivering in the cold, Antonio shook his head. "No."

Brother Francis smiled. "You will. I'm coming to your village of Greccio to celebrate Christmas Eve. It's the holiest night of the year."

Brother Francis sang all the way back to town. His joyful songs of praise wrapped around Antonio's anxious spirit like a warm blanket.

Arriving at the stable, Brother Francis opened a worn leather bag. "I've helped many injured animals. Now *you* can too," he encouraged Antonio. "Mix these herbs with oil and apply them to Benito's wounds. Now don't worry. God loves you *and* the donkey."

"If God really loved me," said Antonio, looking down, "my father would still be alive. And I wouldn't be lame."

"God *does* love you," Brother Francis repeated tenderly, "even when everything seems hopeless. That's the message of Christmas."

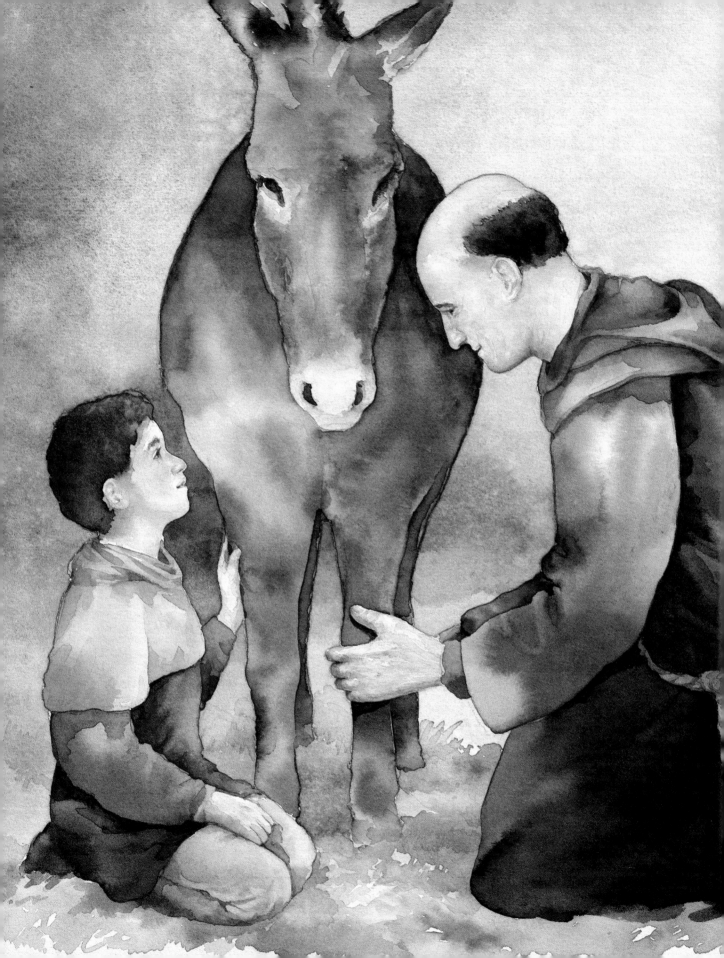

Antonio tossed and turned all night. Finally he went out to the stable and slept next to Benito. Whenever he woke up, he applied herbs on the donkey's wounds.

Early in the morning, Brother Francis arrived. He gently examined Benito while he stroked the donkey's mane. "Benito, *you* are just what I need," he said. Grinning at Antonio, he added, "I need *you*, too."

Antonio shrugged his shoulders. "What for?"

"Help me prepare a surprise for the villagers. I need some hay. And a manger. Could you build one for me?"

Later in the day, Antonio found scraps of wood and began building a manger. "It's too wobbly," he complained to Benito. "The legs aren't right."

Entering the stable again, Brother Francis exclaimed, "Don't give up! It's a work of your heart!" He smiled. "Let's work together and fix it."

Antonio's frustration vanished as they worked side by side.

"Is this manger for another donkey, or a cow?" he asked.

Brother Francis' eyes twinkled.

"Wait and see," he said, getting up to leave. "Just meet me tomorrow at the village square."

When Antonio finished the evening chores, he limped to the room behind the stable where he and his mother lived. *Why does Brother Francis want a manger?* he wondered.

Antonio awoke with a start. *It's Christmas Eve Day!*
He rebandaged Benito's wounds, then hobbled to the village square where
Brother Francis was inviting people to his Christmas Eve celebration.

"Help me, Antonio," urged Brother Francis. "Invite everyone to come
at midnight. We will have a wonderful celebration in the hillside cave."

Antonio knew the villagers felt discouraged by the
recent drought and failed crops. His knees felt weak as he knocked
on the first door. But the more he talked with people, the easier it became.

When Antonio finished inviting the last family, he headed back
home wondering, *Will anyone climb up the hill at midnight?*

That afternoon, Antonio loaded hay along with his manger in a cart and headed up the hill with Brother Francis. A cold wind whipped his clothes as he thought, *I hope my manger holds together.* Out loud, he asked, "Why do you need my manger? Are there animals up here?"

"I have a plan," said Brother Francis. "Just make sure you put a flat rock under the manger's short leg to steady it."

Friends of Brother Francis greeted Antonio when he entered
the warm cave. He looked around and was surprised to see an ox . . .
and Benito! *So that's what the manger is for,* he thought.
"The stablemaster let us use them," explained Brother Francis.
"He said you could return them later. God answered our
prayers—Benito is doing well."

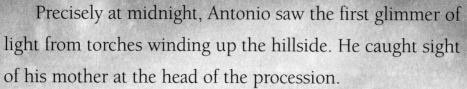

Precisely at midnight, Antonio saw the first glimmer of
light from torches winding up the hillside. He caught sight
of his mother at the head of the procession.

"Antonio!" she called. "Your aunt and uncle just arrived—
with your new cousin!" Antonio's eyes widened
as his aunt handed him her baby.

Brother Francis greeted the couple and said, "God sent you as an answer to my prayers. Could you help me tell the Christmas story? And could we put your baby in Antonio's manger?"

"Yes," they nodded. Brother Francis led them over to the fire.

Carefully cradling his baby cousin, Antonio laid him gently in the manger-bed. "You'll be safe and warm here," he whispered.

A hush fell over the crowd when they arrived at the cave. The two young parents' faces glowed in the flickering firelight. Tiny hands stretched up from the hay. It looked like the Nativity at Bethlehem!

Brother Francis began to read: *"And it came to pass in those days . . . she brought forth her firstborn Son, wrapped Him in swaddling cloths, and laid Him in a manger, because there was no room for them in the inn."*

Brother Francis picked up the baby and said, "The Christ Child of Christmas was born to bring God's gift of forgiveness and eternal life to all people. Jesus set aside His glory in Heaven to become one of us—a baby. He became poor so we could have the riches of God's love. His first home was a barn; His first bed, a manger."

"Ohh!" Antonio whispered to himself. "Baby Jesus slept in a stable, too!"

Brother Francis held the baby close and continued, "Do you wonder where Jesus is when times are hard? He is here. He understands and knows how we feel. And Jesus promised He would never leave us."

Brother Francis motioned for the children to come closer.

Antonio, who usually felt ashamed of his leg, boldly limped out in front.

"I'll teach you a birthday lullaby for Jesus," said Brother Francis.

Thank You, Jesus, Gift of love; You were King of Kings above.

You became a child so small. And You gave Your life for all.

The children joined in the song, and Antonio sang loudest of all.

After many songs of praise ended, everyone thanked Brother Francis. They also thanked Antonio for inviting them. One by one, they headed home with a lightness in their steps, still singing the song they learned that night. The lullaby tune rippled across the wooded hillside. Antonio watched the glowing lights and hummed along.

Brother Francis turned to Antonio. "Thank you, young friend, for *your* part in tonight's celebration. I hope you will continue to help my brothers set up a Christmas Nativity every year."

"I will!" said Antonio. "So will Benito. We could ask the shepherds to come with their sheep, and maybe someone could be the angel."

"Tell me, Antonio, what have you learned about Christmas?"

Antonio rubbed Benito's nose and smiled. "Although I'm poor, God's love makes me rich! And I know Jesus is here to help me. He even helped Benito get well."

Brother Francis smiled and began humming. Antonio added the words, and their praise filled the cave and echoed out into the night.

"*. . .You became a child so small and You gave Your life for all.*"

SAINT FRANCIS OF ASSISI

Saint Francis is one of the most beloved of all saints. As a young man, he gave up a rich inheritance and chose to lead a simple life of serving others. His warm personality, life of extreme poverty, and affection for people and animals inspired many men and women to follow in his footsteps.

We know that his followers made themselves simple, brown robes and built cabins of branches. They sought to live without owning anything, so they could fully concentrate on serving the Lord. Many of them lived in natural caves on steep hillsides. Contrary to the lonely, monastic life of that time, Francis and his followers went forth daily, barefoot and penniless, to preach, nurse the sick, and care for lepers.

Saint Francis spread the love of God throughout his native Italy, and into Spain and Egypt. People of that day felt discouraged, having been ravaged by plagues and war.

Everywhere Francis traveled, he brought hope, joy, and faith to many. He died in 1226 in his middle forties. At the time of his death, the religious order that he founded numbered 5,000 members all over Europe.

Well-known for his singing, Francis composed a new verse for one of his songs even as he lay dying. His joy-filled life of faith, prayer, simplicity, kindness, and serving those in need still inspires many today.

IDEAS for PARENTS and TEACHERS

Plan your own Living Nativity:
Gather dress-up clothes, scarves, and shawls for people and animals.
Build a "manger" of wood or use a cardboard box. Act out the
Christmas story while someone reads sections of Matthew 1 and Luke 1 and 2.
Produce your own living Nativity in your front yard.

Plan a Celebration Party for Jesus' Birthday:
Invite family and neighbors to watch you reenact the events of Jesus' birth.
Bake a birthday cake with one large candle as a reminder of Jesus' words:
"I am the light of the world" John 8:12.
Bake heart-shaped cookies, decorated with red frosting to remind all:
"For God so loved the world that He gave His only begotten Son" John 3:16 NKJV.

Bring Your Gift to Celebrate Jesus' Birth:
Write a poem for Jesus and read it to everyone.
Write a prayer of thanks to God for sending Jesus.
Make up a song to sing in honor of Jesus' birth.
Play instruments and dance in joyful celebration to the Lord.
Draw a picture of the Christmas Nativity.
Make your own Nativity set out of modelling clay.

Nativity Journey:
Beginning on the first of December, set out figurines of a Nativity set.
Begin with Mary and the angel; then add Joseph.
Begin to move them closer to the stable as Christmas nears.
Add Baby Jesus and the shepherds on Christmas Eve.
Keep the three wise men in the distance.
(January 6th is their night of celebration.)

Special Projects:
Make Christmas cards that show and tell the real meaning of Christmas.
Cut up old Christmas cards with Nativity scenes and glue them together as
a collage to hang on a bedroom door.

Additional Bible Readings:
Matthew 1:18-24, Luke 2:1-20, John 1:1-14
Philippians 2:5-11, 1 John 3:16-23, Isaiah 60:1-6